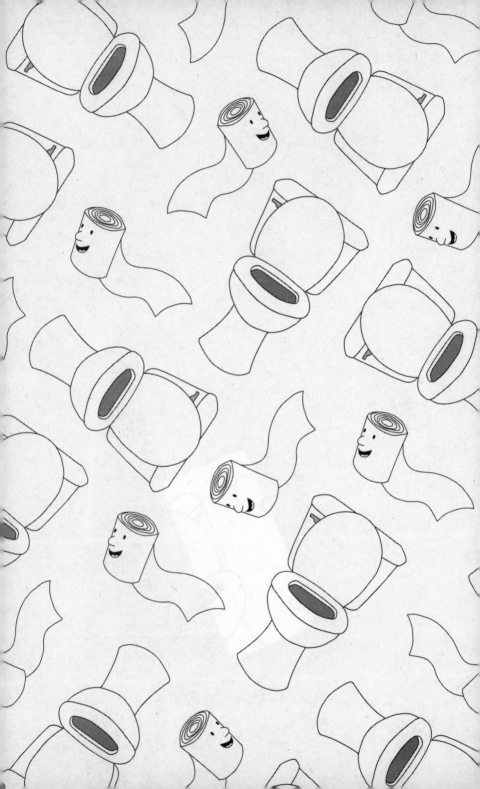

THE JOKIEST JOKING BATHROOM JOKE BOOK EVER WRITTEN . . . NO JOKE!

THE JOKIEST JOKING BATHROOM JOKE BOOK EVER WRITTEN . . . NO JOKE!

1,001 HILARIOUS POTTY JOKES TO MAKE YOU LAUGH WHILE YOU GO

Jokes by May Roche

Illustrations by Amanda Brack

CASTLE POINT BOOKS

NEW YORK

www.stmartins.com
www.castlepointbooks.com

The Castle Point Books trademark is owned by Castle Point Publishing,
LLC.

Castle Point books are published and distributed by St. Martin's Press.

The Library of Congress Cataloging-in-Publication Data is available
upon request.

ISBN 978-1-250-19003-1 (trade paperback)
ISBN 978-1-250-19004-8 (ebook)

Our books may be purchased in bulk for promotional, educational, or
business use. Please contact your local bookseller or the Macmillan
Corporate and Premium Sales Department at 1-800-221-7945, extension
5442, or by email at MacmillanSpecialMarkets@macmillan.com.

First Edition: October 2018

10 9 8 7 6 5 4 3 2 1

For Brendan—

The most propitious, tenacious, pulchritudinous, effervescent, perspicacious, eleemosynary, and chivalrous boy out there.

As you can see I've chosen only the biggest and best words in the dictionary, but they still come up short describing how fantastic you are. They should, however, come in handy the next time you need to beat your father at Scrabble.

CONTENTS

What did the cowboy have to say about his trip to the bathroom?

It was an okie dookie.

How can you distinguish your dad's poop from others?

It's really corny.

Why did the turd never get anything done?

Because he was pooped.

What grows in the ground and smells like poo?

Turdnips.

What do you call a kid with a bad case of the runs?

Down in the dumps.

What's worse than smelling a fart?

Tasting one.

What day of the week should you never use a public restroom?

Splatterday.

What song does the Lone Ranger sing when he goes to the bathroom?

"Take a dump, take a dump, take a dump dump dump . . ."

TYPES OF POOP

- **Jaws:** *Things are quiet at first . . . but then the tension starts to build. Better get outta the water, quick!*

- **The DMV:** *Clear your schedule because this one is going to take ALL DAY.*

- **The Scrubber:** *A poop so big that it cleans your hole on its way out.*

- **Mount Vesuvius:** *Unexpected—and dangerously explosive—diarrhea.*

- **The Ploop:** *When you go and it makes a nice little splash!*

- **The Crayon:** *When it leaves marks in the bowl even after you flush.*

- **The Cookout:** *When there are visible chunks of corn in there.*

• **The False Alarm:** *When you rush to get to a bathroom only to discover it was just a fart.*

• **The Dentist:** *A poop that takes so long and hurts so much it's like pulling teeth.*

• **The Hallelujah:** *When you finally get to poop after being stuck in traffic for an hour . . . and needing to use the bathroom the whole time.*

The Viper: A poop that coils so much that you fear it might strike back out of the toilet.

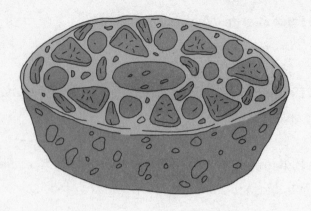

The Fruitcake: The sort of poop
that's such an ordeal that you don't want
to see it again for at least another year.

The Haunted Poop: When you go to the bathroom
in the middle of the night and you're convinced
something might be in the toilet.

What is white, yellow, smooth, and deadly?
A shark-infested toilet

What did the butt cheeks say after they lost the poop?

"It's over between us!"

Why didn't Robin Hood need a toilet?

He had his very own Little John always by his side.

What does the pope do in the bathroom?

Holy crap.

What is a constipated gambler's favorite game?

Craps.

Why did the piece of poop feel so old?

Because he was turning turdy.

What is a dump truck driver's lucky number?

Two.

What's the stinkiest city?

Pitts-burgh.

Why didn't the baseball player have any friends?

Because he'd always try to run home.

What do you call an incompetent accountant's bowel movement?

An income poop.

Why did the kid bring a toilet to the birthday party?
He was a party pooper.

What happened to the man who pooped on the sidewalk?

He was fined for littering.

What do you call a comedian with irritable bowel syndrome?

The life of the potty.

What do you call someone who spends over a half hour in the bathroom each morning?

Dad.

Why do underpants make good detectives?

Because they are good at going undercover.

Why can't nerds vacation at the beach?
Because cats try to bury them in the sand.

What's the crappiest candy?
Reese's feces.

Did you hear about the diarrhea outbreak?
You should have. It's all over town.

Did you hear about the movie *Constipation*?
It was never released.

What's the grossest cookbook ever published?
Dump Dinners.

What does a liar say?
"I didn't fart; it was the seat that made the noise!"

What did the toilet bowl say when Moby Dick took a seat?
"Make way! He's gonna blow!"

What's the difference between a deep-fried wiener and a post-cookout poop?
One is a corn dog, and the other is a corned log.

Did you hear about the guy whose armpits were so smelly that they made his Speed Stick slow down and reconsider?

What's the most disgusting kids' book ever written?
Diarrhea of a Wimpy Kid.

Where should you never step on a baseball diamond?

Turd base.

What's the difference between a museum and a chili cook-off?

One is artsy, and the other is fartsy.

Student: *Teacher, can I go to the bathroom?*
Teacher: *No, no. May I go to the bathroom?*
Student: *Hey, I asked first!*

What has nine siblings and smells like poo?

A finger.

Why did the guy get poop on his phone?

He was playing "Turds with Friends."

What's another name for the world's biggest toilet?

A swimming pool.

What grows in the ground, smells like poo, and can be made into French fries?
Poo-tatoes.

Did you hear the joke about the toilet?
It's pretty filthy!

What's another name for a skunk?
A fart squirrel.

Why do police officers sit down when they go to the bathroom?
It's the best way to do their duty.

What do you have after you eat a prune pizza?
Pizzeria!

What do you give an elephant with diarrhea?
Room.

Why are constipated old men so rude?
Because they don't give a crap.

What does Scooby-Doo do after eating Scooby Snacks?
Scooby doodie doo.

What do you call someone using an army latrine?
A pooper trooper.

What's cute, furry, and eats cat poop?

A dog.

Did you hear about the guy that pooped in his sleep?

He took too many Tylenol BMs.

What did the crap say to the fart?

You blow me away.

What did the toilet order at McDonalds?

A number 2.

Why didn't the monster flush the toilet?

He didn't need to. He scared the crap out of it.

Why was the security guard standing on dog poop?

He was on duty.

Why did Beethoven go to the bathroom in the woods?

Because he wanted his poop to decompose.

Why won't vampires feast on joggers?
They give them the runs.

What did the man fly say to the lady fly?

Excuse me, is this stool taken?

Why do toilets love jokes so much?
Because they are always down in the dumps.

Why wouldn't the baseball player use public toilets?

Because he liked home runs.

What's brown, smells horrid, and got all over the king's horses and king's men?

Humpty's dump.

Real movies that sound like something you would do in the bathroom:

Splash
Free Willy
Fire Down Below
What Lies Beneath
That Thing You Do
Unfinished Business
Goldfinger
Private Parts
Sudden Impact
Peewee's Big Adventure
Hot Fuzz
Blown Away
Forces of Nature
The Remains of the Day
Children of the Corn
Gone with the Wind
The Blob
Dirty Work
Something's Gotta Give

John: *What is purple, has spikes, and can sing a beautiful tune?*

Lou: *I don't know. What?*

John: *A dookie.*

Lou: *What? A dookie is none of those things!*

John: *I know. I just wanted to make the riddle difficult to solve.*

What did the food poisoning do to the man's bowels?

It rectum.

What did the serial killer do to the toilet?

He murdered it.

What do you call a telephone worker who took too many laxatives?

A smooth operator.

Did you hear about the jogger looking for the bathroom?

He had the runs.

Why did the car with a dead battery and the constipated kid have in common?

Neither one could go.

What is the worst air freshener to have in the bathroom?

Poo-pourri

What do you call a toilet wearing a fuzzy seat cover?

A costume potty.

What's frozen, falls from the sky, and stinks?

Hail-itosis.

Did you hear about the redhead whose breath stinks?
Her dentist said it because she had ginger-vitis.

Do you want to hear a secret?
Is it that you have bad breath? That's no secret.

What do you call poop on a stick?
Shish-ka-poop.

How does poop surf the internet?
They log on.

What's tight, white, and full of holes?

Dad's underwear.

One way to tell you've got bad breath:

You ask a friend for a piece of gum and they hand you a roll of toilet paper.

2
QUICK PICKS

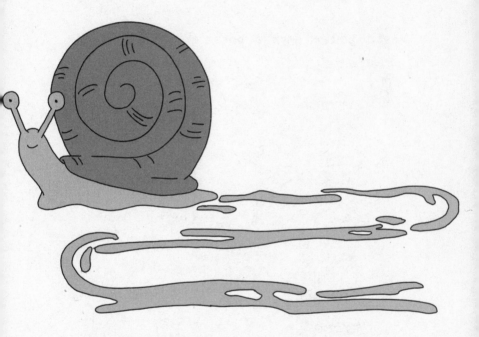

The Snail: A long slimy trail of snot.

What do boogers and nerds have in common?

People like to pick on them.

What's a nose's favorite movie?

Boogie Nights

What do you call a wall of boogers?

A picket fence.

What's full of boogers and smells?

A nose.

Did you hear about the booger who liked to gossip?

He was pretty nosy.

What's the difference between boogers and Brussels sprouts?

No one eats Brussels sprouts.

Why did the little boy only eat boogers?

He was a picky eater.

What do you call a booger that's been on a diet?

Slim Pickins.

Did you hear the nose got back together with a bunch of snot?

It was an old phlegm.

What did the ear overhear the other ear saying?
There's something between us that smells.

TYPES OF SNOT

• **Chunky Monkey:** *When you have hard boogers stuck on top of slimy boogers.*

• **The Phantom:** *When you pick one and it just . . . disappears.*

• **The Nose Dandruff:** *A dry, flaky booger that just kind of falls out of your nose of its own volition.*

• **The Fugitive:** *A booger that you just can't seem to grab, and it gets farther and farther up there and out of reach.*

• **Dracula's Delight:** *Bloody boogers.*

• **The Clinger:** *A booger that just won't come loose, no matter how hard you try.*

• **Tenacious B:** *A booger that you try to flick away, but it won't budge, or even worse, it moves over to the other finger you're using to flick it off.*

• **The Old-Timer:** *A booger that's so old and dry that it's gone from green to gray.*

• **The Trophy:** *A booger so big that took you so long to get out that you kind of want to show it off to everybody.*

• **The Mysterious Cave:** *When you pick your nose because it's irritated and there aren't any boogers or snot in there at all.*

What does a booger say to his girlfriend?
I'm stuck on you.

The Broken Faucet: When you've got a cold or allergies and you lean over and a bunch of snot just pours right out of your nose.

Where do boogers go on vacation?

Snotland!

Why do we have fingernails?

So we can dig deeper!

What do you say to your friend when they're hungry?

Go to Booger King.

What do you get if you put peppers in your nose?

A hot boogie.

Why did the booger and the pimple team up?

They were sick of being picked on!

Why is there no such thing as an empty nose?

Because even a clean one has fingerprints.

Did you hear about the guy who could pick his nose, dance, and play the trumpet all at the same time?

They called him the Boogie Woogie Bugle Boy.

What button stinks most?

A belly button.

Why did the loogey die of old age?

Because slime flies!

Did you hear about the guy whose nose ran for three months straight?

Snot funny.

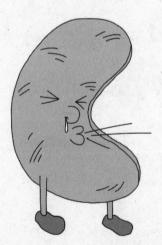

Which nut has the worst allergies?

Cashew.

Where can you find someone who's never picked their nose?

Nowhere. That person has never existed.

How are boogers and fruits similar?

Both get picked and eaten.

What did the booger say when the magician asked for a volunteer?

Pick me! Pick me!

What do noses and apple pies have in common with each other?

They're both crusty.

What monster can stick to walls?

The boogeyman.

What did the booger's dad say to his son when he talked back?

Don't be snotty with me!

What's thick, slimy, and hangs from tall trees?

Giraffe snot.

What was the nose so melancholy about?

It didn't get picked.

What's inside of a haunted spirit's nose?

Booogers.

What do you call a ball of snot wearing a motorcycle helmet?

A snail!

What's yellow, sticky, and smells like bananas?

Monkey snot.

What's a booger's favorite casino in Vegas?

The Golden Nugget.

What do you call the biggest booger in the world?

Green Giant.

Fancy Words for Boogers (for when you need to be dignified about your bodily functions)

Nostril Pickings

Gold Dust

Hidden Gems

Upper Crusts

Boogeaux

Nasal Soil

What do noses and brie cheese have in common?

They both smell and get runny.

What do you call a Roman emperor with a cold?

Julius Sneezer.

What did the kid say to the booger?

It's been nice gnawing you.

Why did John hate his nose?

Because it didn't smell very good.

What do toenails and cheese have in common?

Their smell.

Who is the snottiest writer?

Ian Phleming.

What did the gross magician say when he picked at his pimple?

Scabracadabra!

What did the finger do when the nose went on strike?

Picket.

What runs in most families?

Noses.

What is dandruff's favorite cereal?

Anything with flakes.

A little boy picked his nose, then licked his finger. His father noticed him doing it and said, "Son, stop that! That is absolutely disgusting!" Then he took a tissue and wiped the booger off is finger. "Hey, I should be the one mad at you," the boy said. "And why is that?" his father asked. "I didn't get to flick it, and that's the most fun part!"

What is another name for snowman dandruff?

Frosted Flakes.

What did the diabetic woman find in her nose?

A sugar booger.

What is a gross boy's favorite food?

Hamboogers.

Why was the nose so excited?

Because it was time to boo-gie woogie.

What do you leave a for a waiter whose
ears are full of gunk?

A Q-tip.

Did you hear about the girl with too much earwax?

It was downright ear-ie.

What's the best part about flossing your teeth?

Finding all the free snacks for later!

What do zits drink?

Pop.

What do you call a little zit?

A simple pimple.

What do Italian teenagers eat?

Zit-i.

Why should you not worry when you get a pimple?

Because zit happens.

Did you hear about the really tall guy with dandruff?

The mayor thought it was snowing and
ordered the schools canceled.

Why didn't anyone want to hang out with Dandruff Dave?

He was really flaky.

I remember when my ears used to be a lot filthier.

Sorry, I was just waxing nostalgic.

Did you hear about the guy who had a massive waxy buildup in his head?

It was earful, just earful!

What's worse than having an ear full of earwax?

Having an ear full of earwigs.

What do you do if you see a hardworking booger?

Pick it!

EAR WAX MONIKERS

- *Sticky icky.*

- *Ear turds.*

- *Headphone honey.*

- *Witches' butter.*

What's the difference between a banana and a pimple?

One bruises easily, the other oozes easily.

What did the pimple say to the butt?

"I'm tired of people picking on us!"

What's another name for a slug?

Look in your nose.

What do mean girls do to dandruff?

Give it the cold shoulder.

Why did the environmentalist use so much mouthwash?

He wanted to fight air pollution.

What did the bro say to the witch?

"Wart's up?"

3
BUTT, WHY?

What soda do butts like best?

Squirt.

Why are only the cleanest butts allowed to sing solos?

Because they are soap-ranos.

What do you call an old butt that has seen it all?

A wise crack.

Where do butts buy their groceries?

Hole Foods.

What do butts and lasers have in common?

They both go "pew-pew"!

What music band do butts like best?

Tom Petty and the Fart Breakers.

What is the grossest reality show?

Shart Tank.

What do butts eat at the movies?

Poopcorn.

What's the worst thing someone
can do in the bathroom?

Mix up the toilet brush for a toothbrush.

What's another name for panda poop?

Endangered feces.

What do you get when you put a turd in the freezer?

A poopsicle.

What do you get after eating too much ice cream?

A chocolate swirl.

What did the guy get when he couldn't make it to the bathroom in time?

Heavy pants.

What's the worst thing you can do in the laundry room?

Mistake the dryer for a toilet.

What basketball team can't control their bowels?

The San Antonio Spurts.

How many logs can you fit in an empty toilet?

One. After that, it isn't empty anymore.

Why did the pastry chef use jalapeños?

He wanted to ensure his buns were hot.

What did one fireman say to the other in the bathroom?

Fire in the hole!

What's worse than finding a fly in your soup?

Finding a fly in your poop.

What do you get after eating too many Oreos?

Cookie dookie.

Why was the mathematician's bowel movement so upsetting?

Because it had a lot of problems.

Did you hear this book is a #2 bestseller?

Why was the ditch digger so constipated?
He was a mud clutcher.

What was the constipated librarian doing in the bathroom?
Working on the backlog.

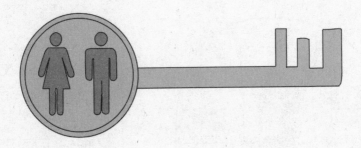

What do you use to unlock the bathroom door?
A doo-key.

What did the comedian say when he looked at his poop?

Yuk yuk.

How did the toilet paper hit the jackpot
in a game of slots?

It was on a roll.

When is the most satisfying time to go to the bathroom?

Poo thirty!

Where is the most painful place to go number two on a car trip?

A fork in the road.

What do you get after eating too many blueberries?

Smurf poop.

What place did the piece of poop get in the race?

Turd place.

What do you never appreciate until it's gone?
Toilet paper.

What's brown, sticky, and sounds like a clock tower?

Dung.

How do you get your butt to wipe itself?
Eat toilet paper.

How is a butt like the Liberty Bell?

They both have a big crack.

What happens after you eat too much alphabet soup?

You get really bad vowel movements.

When is laughter the worst medicine?

When you have diarrhea.

What is another name for Eskimo poop?

Pudding-pops.

FOUL LANGUAGE

Believe it or not, these are real quotes—because even the most interesting people in history love to talk about what we do in the bathroom.

"Everybody looks at their poop."
—Oprah Winfrey

"Always go to the bathroom when you have a chance."
—King George V

"Home is where the heart is, home is where the fart is."
—Ernest Hemingway

"Fart for freedom, fart for liberty—and fart proudly."
—Benjamin Franklin

"An employer's fart is music to his employees' ears."
—Mokokoma Mokhonoana

"You failed—your fart was not silent, my nose heard its deafening noise."
—Aniekee Tochukwu Ezekiel

"My trumpeting sounds like a goose farting in the fog."
—Alex O'Loughlin

"You are all made of real poop."
—Anne Frank

"Men who consistently leave the toilet seat up secretly want women to get up to go to the bathroom in the middle of the night and fall in."
—Rita Rudner

What's worse than a big juicy fart coming out of your butt?
A big juicy fart going into your butt.

What do you call a poop that comes out really slooooooow?
A turdle.

What did the guy say after he made a square poop?
"Ouch."

Why did the cook wipe his butt before he pooped?
He liked to make things from scratch.

fahrvergnügen: **A German word that means "driving pleasure."**

fahrompüpen A German word for constipation.

What's the one thing in the world that feels even better than being in love?

Finding a clean toilet when you're out in public when diarrhea strikes.

What do a spaceship and toilet paper have in common?

They both probe Uranus.

What's the easiest way to lose two pounds?

Drop off a deuce in the bathroom.

How was the boy able to fart so loudly that it fell on a thousand ears?

He did it in a cornfield.

What did the surfer say in the bathroom?

Wipe out!

Why did the clarinet player smell so bad?

She was always practicing her wind instrument.

Why did the secretary stay in the bathroom for so long?

Because no job is finished until the paperwork is done.

A little boy in church needed to go to the bathroom. "Mom, can I go take a dump?" he asked. "Yes," his mother replied, "but we're in church. Next time don't say 'dump,' say 'whisper.' It's more polite." The next Sunday, the boy is sitting by his father, and again he needed to use the bathroom. "Dad, I have to whisper," the boy said. "Okay," the father replied. "Whisper in my ear."

I tried to follow Constipation on Twitter, but got blocked.

Why did the man poop on his lawn?

He was too cheap to buy fertilizer.

Why did the salesman poop in the furniture store?

Because the customer asked to see a stool sample.

What's another name for a poop that floats?

Bob.

Why did the woman put plastic wrap
on the toilet seat?

She wanted to seal in the freshness.

Why did the King stay on his throne?

He was constipated.

What do you do when you find blue poop in the toilet?

Try to cheer it up.

Did you hear about the author who couldn't poop for a week?

Talk about a bad case of writer's block.

Where does the government keep all the most valuable farts?

Fart Knox.

What's the most unpopular activity at summer camp?

Farts and Crafts.

Why are farts worse than bad breath?

Because you can at least put a mint in your mouth.

What's a toilet's favorite kind of frozen yogurt?

Chocolate swirl.

What does an umpire say after he takes a poop?

"You're out!"

What does the lifeguard say after he goes to the bathroom?

"Everybody out of the pool!"

POO-PHEMISMS

- *Coaching the Browns*

- *Dropping the lobster in the water*

- *Drowning a rat*

- *Feeding the porcelain puppy*

- *Cutting bait*

- *Freeing the hostages*

- *Making mud pies*

- *Putting the meat loaf in the oven*

- *Logging on*

- *Letting some air out of the tires*

- *Making a doo-posit*

- *Baking brownies*

- *Crowning a new king of Brownland*

- *Checking in on breakfast*

- *I got an anaconda who don't wanna be in my buns, hon*

- *Wink at the toilet for an extended period of time*

- *Back that thang up*

- *Baiting the trap*

- *Bombing the porcelain sea*

- *Helping the beavers build a dam*

- *Going to play **Call of Doody***

What soda tastes like prunes?

Dr. Pooper.

Have you seen *Howard's End*?

You probably shouldn't. That's where his poop comes from!

Did you hear M. Night Shyamalan directed a movie about an impacted colon?

There was a twist at the end.

What is the stinkiest palindrome?

POOP.

What's worse than finding fake poop in your bed?

Finding real poop in your bed.

Did you hear about the guy who desperately stumbled into the bathroom in the middle of the night and couldn't find the toilet?

It was a shart in the dark.

Why did the dad only change his baby's diaper one time?

The box said up to 20 pounds.

A 60-year-old, a 70-year-old, and an 80-year-old were all playing bingo when the 60-year-old said, "Being 60 is the worst age. I sit on the toilet all day and I can't pee at all!"

"That's nothing," said the 70-year-old. "I can't even poop!"

"No," said the 80-year-old. "I have the worst age."

"Do you have trouble peeing?" the 60-year-old asked.

"No, not at all. Every day at 6 a.m."

"What about pooping?" the 70-year-old asked.

"Not a problem. 6:30 a.m.," he said.

"So you're telling me," the 70-year-old said, "that you have the hardest age, but you can pee and poop easily? What's the problem?"

"The problem is that I don't get up till 8 o'clock."

How is your younger sibling like a diaper?

They're always full of it, and always on your butt.

What did the rectum say was its relationship status on Facebook?

"It's constipated."

What's green, hairy, has three legs and smells horrible?

I don't know either. But I found it in the toilet!

Why shouldn't you buy shampoo?

It's fake. Get real poo.

Bill: *How do you define messy?*

John: *Dirty and unorganized?*

Bill: *No, the bathroom after you get done with it!*

What did the worried mom leave in the toilet?

A nervous wreck.

Bill: *Did you have corn for lunch?*

John: *Yes, how did you know?*

Bill: *You forgot to flush the toilet.*

What do you call a supermodel with a bad case of diarrhea?

A hot mess.

What happens after you eat peppers?

They get jalapeño dirty business.

Did you hear about the basketball player who had diarrhea?

He got called out for double-dribbling.

What flower do you give someone
who overcomes constipation?

A ploppie!

What did the toilet say on *Wheel of Fortune*?

I'd like to buy a bowel, please!

Did you hear about the guy who posted online every time he pooped?

He had a log blog.

Did you hear about the man who didn't poop for months and then got diarrhea?

Talk about a blast from the past.

Did you hear about the high school kid who pooped out a misshapen log in total silence?

It was a teenage mutant ninja turdle.

Police: *Sir, please open the door and come out immediately.*
Man: *But I'm pooping!*
Police: *Yes, but you're in a taxi.*

Did you hear about the new album by the band Diarrhea?

It leaked early.

Which Pokémon can't control its bowels?

Squirtle.

What kind of pants can you poop in?
Dungarees.

What happens if you eat too many Mexican jumping beans?

Your poop will jump right out of the toilet.

On which carnival ride is it okay to poop your pants?

The dumper cars.

What's brown and spins around your waist?

A hula poop.

4
SLIGHTLY IRREGULAR

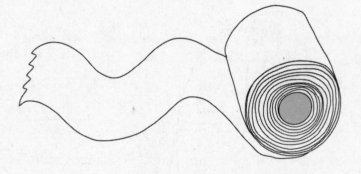

What's on a roll but doesn't have any wheels?

Toilet paper.

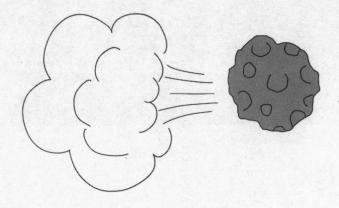

A shooting star is just another name for a farting comet.

DID YOU KNOW

• *A fart is just a secret your butt whispers to your underwear.*

• *True happiness is getting to use your own toilet again after being away on vacation.*

• *Farting is like letting the wind out of your own sails.*

• *Farting is like letting go of a bad memory—if it stays with you, it'll poison you.*

• *Farting is like eating an entire bag of sour candy—do it, and before you know it, way worse things are coming.*

• *Farting is playing a high-stakes game of chicken with a fart.*

• *Farting is the original air mail.*

• *Farting is just your body making thunder before the lightning.*

• *Farting is just your butt being jealous of your talking, singing mouth.*

• *Farting is a literal example of somebody butting into the conversation.*

• *Pooping is just having one last goodbye with a meal you truly loved.*

• *A poop is just a fart that worked hard and applied itself.*

• *Farting while you're eating is just a "coming attraction."*

What do you call a stinky postman?

Mail-odious.

What five words can strike fear into the heart of even the strongest, toughest brute?

"Turn your head and cough."

What drink is both disgusting and refreshing?

Cherry Slimeade.

What do you call it when you fart glitter?

Very interesting.

What kind of shoes do plumbers hate the most?

Clogs.

PLUMB CRAZY

What's the best name for a plumber?

Dwayne.

What is a plumber's favorite amusement park ride?

The log flume.

What should a plumber never bring to a potluck?

Beef stew.

Did you hear about Paul, the greatest plumber in the world? Don't talk to him.

He's pooped.

Where do rainbows use the bathroom?

In pots o´gold!

Why was the decapitated head so lonely?

He had no body to be with.

What would be the worst insect
to be reincarnated as?

A stinkbug.

What's the stickiest kind of jazz music?

Scat.

What do you call a pixie that needs a bath?

Stinker Belle.

What do you call going to the bathroom on an RV?

Going on the go!

What do you get if you cross a witch with a constellation?
Star Warts.

What do you call a guy who makes armpit farts all night?
A pit orchestra musician.

What kind of toilets can you buy at a drugstore?
Toilet-trees.

A fart is like a speech—it's not what you say, it's how you say it.

Two boys go into two bathroom stalls, and finish at about the same time. The first boy goes to the sink to wash his hands. The second boy is about to leave, and the first boy asks, "Aren't you going to wash your hands? I was taught to always wash my hands after using the bathroom." The second boy laughed and said, "Well, I was taught not to pee on my hands," and he left.

Why shouldn't you take Pokémon into the bathroom when you need to go?
They might Pikachu.

What do you get when you eat a candy bar, throw it up, take it to a cabin in the woods, and then eat the candy bar again?

A retreat.

What's the worst part about being a cowboy who rides around on a horse all day?

Rawhide.

What do you get when you leave an old pair of underwear outside during a full moon?

An underwearwolf.

What do you call a kid that crosses the road twice but refuses to take a bath?

A dirty double-crosser.

What's the difference between lice and dandruff?

Dandruff has almost no taste at all.

Why did the fleas leave the dirty, disgusting kid alone?

The lice had already called dibs.

What do you get when you cross a skunk with bells?

Jingle smells.

What drink will always make you burp?

Belch's Grape Juice.

What is grosser than a number two after lunch at an all-you-can-eat buffet?

Not much.

What is cool, white, and has a bottom at the top?

A toilet.

What did the roll of toilet paper say to the toilet?

Nothing, toilet paper doesn't talk!

What's the grossest-tasting bean?

Dung beans.

Look, guys, PMS jokes aren't funny. Period.

What's the smelliest ninja turtle?

Leo-farto!

Did you hear about the guy who got lost in the bathroom?

He took a wrong turd.

Did you hear about the thieves who took all the toilets from the police station?

The detectives have nothing to go on.

What's the smelliest retail store?

Walfart.

DIRTY SLOGANS

Just what are these household brands trying to say?

The Juice Is Loose (Starburst)

It's Gonna Move Ya (Juicy Fruit)

It Takes a Tough Man to Make a Tender Chicken (Purdue)

If It Doesn't Get All Over the Place It Doesn't Belong on Your Face (Carl's Jr.)

It Takes a Licking and Keeps on Ticking (Timex)

What Can Brown Do for You? (UPS)

Melts in Your Mouth, Not in Your Hand (M&Ms)

Plop, Plop, Fizz Fizz. Oh, What a Relief It Is. (Alka Seltzer)

It's Finger Lickin' Good (KFC)

Is It Wet or Is It Dry? (Mr. Clean)

Once You Pop You Can't Stop (Pringles)

Real Places That Sound Filthy

Middelfart, Denmark

Tooting Station, UK

Drain, Oregon

Blowhard, Australia

Ta Ta Creek, Canada

Weener, Germany

Greasy, Oklahoma

Butteville, Oregon

Anus, France

Bumpass, Virginia

Titisee, Germany

Tightsqueeze, Virginia

Fanny, West Virginia

Boody, Illinois

Loose Creek, Missouri

Why did the cowboy have to poop standing up?

Because a cowboy should never squat while wearing spurs.

Did you hear about the man who would only bathe in the spring?

He was incredibly smelly because people should bathe in all seasons.

Why are people who pee a lot so laid back?

Because they go with the flow.

What stinks, is covered in mold,
and doesn't belong in the bathroom?

Cheese.

What do you call a vampire that only dines on pigs?
A hampire.

I'm white like milk but you wouldn't want to drink me. What am I?

A toilet.

What's the worst thing to find in your freezer?

Frozen pees.

What's the difference between apple juice and pee?

A kid will wash their hands if they get covered in apple juice.

What is the moon's favorite song
to sing in the bathroom?

Tinkle, Tinkle Little Star.

I'm a bowl but you wouldn't want to
eat cereal out of me. What am I?

A toilet.

What's the grossest device to listen to music with?
An iPood.

What's yellow, has spiked hair, and smells awful?
Fart Simpson.

What's another name for monster barf?
Goulash.

How can you find the bathroom in France?

Check with the mon-sewer.

Why did the bum interrupt the speech?

Because he liked to butt in.

What did Rudolph say to Santa when his bathroom break lasted too long?

Can you wrap it up in there?

What do you call someone who is obsessed with toilet jokes?

A commodian.

What's the worst way to get your feet dirty?

When you mix up your thong underwear with your thong sandals.

Did you hear that the guy who sang "Baby" and "Love Yourself" drank too much soda before he got on his tour bus and wound up urinating in his pants?

Poor Justin Pee-ber.

What's the difference between a clock and a toilet?

One is a time machine,
and the other is a grime machine.

What should you never order in a French restaurant?

Poofflé.

Who shouts "tee-hee" when you poke him in the stomach . . . and then makes a huge mess?

Poopin' Fresh.

Toilets really like it when you're polite, so make sure to say your pees and thank-poos.

Did you hear about the kid who had to give a report and hid in the bathroom?

He was stalling.

What's the only TV show you can watch in the bathroom?

Game of Thrones.

What do baby mailmen deliver?

Packages that are packed and loaded.

Did you hear about the lactose-intolerant comedian?

He's great; none of his jokes are cheesy.

John Swifties

"I didn't make it to the bathroom in time," John burst out.

"I shouldn't have waited so long to clean the toilet," John said crustily.

"The bulb burst in the bathroom and I couldn't see what I was doing," John said delightedly.

"I pooped so hard I think my colon fell out!" said John, feeling disorganized.

"Better get some air circulating in here fast, it stinks!" John said fanatically.

"I installed the new toilet!" John said, flushed with success.

"I'm having some pretty bad diarrhea today," John gushed.

"Honestly, it makes me want to vomit," was John's gut reaction.

"Don't you have anything to get rid of the smell in here?" John asked, incensed.

"Why is my voice so raspy?" John asked phlegmatically.

"I couldn't hold it in any longer!" John leaked.

"I finished cleaning out the septic tank," John said successfully.

"I have flow issues," John sputtered.

"While this over here is a toilet seat," John went on.

"These jokes make me wanna barf," John said wretchedly.

Where's the best place to buy toilet paper?

Just find it on Poo-gle.

When you use a toilet on the airplane, where does the poop go?

Nowhere—they never clean those toilets.

How are socks like diapers?

They should be changed frequently.

5
WHEN A FART ISN'T A FART

What do ninjas and farts have in common?
They are both silent and deadly.

Why did the conductor fart so loud?

He wanted to toot his own horn.

What do you call passing gas in a pair of borrowed pants?

A fart transplant.

Why do teenagers fart so much?

Because it is the only gas they can afford.

What do you call a person who is too shy to fart in public?

A private tooter.

Q: *Why don't farts graduate from high school?*

A: *Because they always end up getting expelled.*

How can you tell if a person has a good imagination?

They think their farts smell good.

What is the stinkiest country?

Fargentina.

What do a bowl of chili and a filling station have in common?

They both give you gas.

What can go right through your pants and not leave a hole?

A fart.

The Flamingo : A fart so substantial that you have to stand on one leg to help it get out.

The Organ Grinder: That rare fart that comes out in multiple tones that it sounds like you're playing a jaunty, old-timey tune.

TYPES OF FARTS

Farts come in all shapes and sizes. Have you ever experienced any of these?

• **The Crescendo:** *A fart that starts quiet . . . but that just keeps getting LOUDER.*

• **The Déjà vu:** *When you swear you've smelled something just like it before, somewhere, sometime.*

• **The Trapper Keeper:** *The hostile act of a fart in an enclosed space, like a compact car or an elevator.*

• **The Zombie:** *When a fart smells so nasty that you're sure you're dead and are slowly rotting from the inside out.*

• **The Rapid Fire:** *A bunch of farts all at once that make a rat-tat-tat-tat-tat sound, like you're a machine gunner on a warship.*

• **The Odorless Wonder:** *A fart that's all noise and no smell, but still somehow just as embarrassing.*

• **Flavor Country:** *A fart so nasty that you don't just smell it, but you taste it a little, too.*

• **The Bubbler:** *A fart sneakily emitted in a bathtub or hot tub that just looks like a bigger bubble.*

• **The Whodunit:** *A silent but stinky fart in a crowded place . . . but only you know who was responsible. (It was* **you!***)*

• **The Drowned Out:** *A fart let loose in a place so loud—a concert, a sporting event, a dance club—that nobody knows you did it.*

• **The Forgiven:** *A fart in church that nobody is going to call you out for.*

• **The Mosquito Bite:** *A fart that hurts just a little bit.*

• **The Fair Warning:** *It may feel, sound, and smell like a simple fart, but you understand it for what it is: a two-minute warning to get to the bathroom . . . and fast.*

Where do ghost farts come from?
Booooooooooties.

Did you hear about the guy that ate an entire bowl of baked beans before going to the ballet?

He shouldn't have.

Did you hear about the girl that was in love with the smell of her own farts?

She was inflatuated.

What's the difference between the
Mona Lisa and passing gas?

One is a work of art. One is a work of fart.

Did you hear about the couple that were perfect for each other?

She was a heartbreaker and he was a fart-breaker.

How can a fart surprise you?

If it's got a lump in it.

What do you call a group of superheroes after a chili competition?

The fartastic four.

If you're an odious gas, life begins at farty.

Why does a black hole never fart?

Because nothing can escape it!

Where's the best place to buy beans?
At the gas station.

Where do farts go skating?

At the roller stink.

What do you call a fart you make in the laundry room?

A fluffy.

Did you hear about the prince who ate too many beans?

It resulted in noble gas.

Did you hear about the fart joke book?

It was a best smeller!

What do you call a baby's fart?

Little stinker.

Did you hear about the incident at the bean factory?

There was a gas leak.

How many teenagers does it take to stink up a room?

Only a phew.

Did you hear about the fart factory that not only made farts but also sold them?

Their motto was, "Whoever smelt it, dealt it."

What University smells the worst?

P.U.

How does a cow's fart smell?

Udderly terrible.

A fart is just a poop . . .

• *that doesn't believe in itself.*

• *that's honking for your butthole to get out of the way.*

• *calling to let you know he's running late.*

• *sounding the evacuation alarm.*

What's the stinkiest piece of clothing?
A windbreaker.

Did you hear about the boy who couldn't stop farting in class?

He was a-gassed!

What do you call a Mozart fart?

Classical gas.

What smells worse? A burp or a fart?

Hard to say, but together they could knock out a horse.

What did the brave man do?

Took a chance on a fart after a day of diarrhea.

Why do farts smell so bad?

So your deaf Grandpa can enjoy them too!

Why shouldn't you fart in an Apple store?

They don't have Windows.

Why won't vampires feast on weathermen?

They give them wind.

How do you know it's time to go to the bathroom?

When the coffee cup's empty.

What did the astronaut say before he farted?

Blast off!

What do you call a vegan with diarrhea?

A salad shooter.

How do you make still water turn to sparkling?

Easy, just fart in the glass!

I didn't fart. That was just my bowels blowing you a kiss!

Why was the surfer scared to go into the water?

Farts were circling.

Why was the RV so stinky?
Because it was full of gas.

License to Smell

Some people love bathroom humor so much they have to take it on the road!

• *LUV2FRT*

• *IFRTID*

• *IGOTTAP*

• *RNONGAS*

- *KSMYGAS*

- *OLDFRT*

- *PASNGAS*

- *ICUP*

- *LUVSHARTZ*

- *BUTKISR*

- *STOLBUS*

- *TURDLE*

- *DIDUFRT*

- *NVRFLSH*

- *BGDMP*

- *EATMCRP*

- *EATMGAS*

- H8FARTS

- GOT2POO

- JCYPOO

What do stinky kids eat for breakfast?
Pooptarts.

John: *What's the best way to catch a fart?*
Lou: *Why would anyone want to catch a fart?*

TOP 5 BEST PLACES TO FART

- *Walking past first-class boarding a plane.*

- *In the library next to a rude person who is being too loud.*

- *In an elevator if you were riding with someone who didn't return a hello.*

- *When someone cuts in line behind you.*

- *In your coach's office. After you've just been cut from the team.*

Why did Pocahontas eat a bag of fruity jelly beans and then fart?

Because she wanted to paint with all the colors of the wind.

What did the lady with a run in her stockings do?

She got to a bathroom, quick!

Why can you only put 359 beans in a soup?

Because one more would make it "Too Farty!"

Want to know an easy way to transform your tub into a jacuzzi?

Take a bath after eating broccoli casserole.

Did you hear about the lost fart?

He turned into a burp.

Why did the teenager finally quit farting?

He ran out of gas.

What is rude, can travel through solid material, and can bring you to tears?

Farts.

Sunday	Monday	Tootsday	Wednesday	Thursday	Friday	Saturday
3	4	5	6	7	8	9

What is the stinkiest day of the week?

Tootsday.

Did you hear about the fart that went on an adventure?

It made a great escape!

Why did the woman pass gas in the elevator?
She wanted to take her farts to a new level.

Why did the boy fart in the cemetery?
Because he read a tombstone that said RIP.

How did the ninja hide his fart?
He masked it.

Why are farts so wholesome?
Because it's what's on the inside that counts.

Did you hear about the kid who just turned 10 and ate too much prune cake?
He turned his birthday party into a birthday farty.

In space, no one can hear you fart . . . and if you're wearing a spacesuit, only you can smell it.

What causes cold winter winds?
Frosty, after eating a bowl of chili.

What's green and smells like flies?

Kermit's farts.

What do you get when you fart in a shepherd's pie?

Never invited over for dinner again.

Little Johnny: *Mom! Dad! I was the only kid that knew the answer to the question the teacher asked today!*

Mom: *That's wonderful! What was the question?*

Little Johnny: *Who farted?*

What kind of pizza smells like farts?

Smell-eroni pizza.

What happens when you cross an atomic bomb with beans?

A weapon of gas destruction!

Have you heard about the new line of Fartphones?

I wouldn't buy one. They're real stinkers.

Did you hear about the bad student with bad gas?

He kept getting farter behind, so his parents hired him a tooter.

Why can't farts get a decent education?

Because they always get expelled.

What do you call a monkey that farts in church?

A badboon.

Why did the rooster call in sick?

He had the cock-a-doodle-flu.

Did you hear about the lion with diarrhea?

It was a cat-astrophe.

How can you tell the difference between elephant and rhinoceros poop?

Elephants work for peanuts.

Why don't monkeys get constipated?
Because they are always in the swing of things.

Why do lap dogs have the worst-smelling poop?

Because they are so spoiled.

What does a dog call a litter box?

All-you-can-eat buffet.

What do dogs call fire hydrants?

Public toilets.

Did you hear the joke about squirrel poop?

It was really nutty.

What is the most difficult animal to hold
a conversation with?

A goat because they always butt in.

Why did the chicken cross the road?
To get to the bathroom.

What's invisible and smells like bananas?
Monkey farts.

What dog has the most germs?
Bac-terrier.

What do a race track and your little brother's underwear have in common?

They're both covered in skid marks.

Why did the armadillo cross the road?

To show that he had guts.

Why do worms make good detectives?

They know how to get to the bottom of things.

Where does a baseball player rub toilet paper?

On his bat.

What do you get when a cat has a cold?

Mew-cus.

A bear and a rabbit are pooping in the woods. The bear asked the rabbit, "Do you have problems with poop sticking to your fur? The rabbit, a little confused, replied, "No." "That's great!" said the bear as he grabbed the rabbit and started wiping.

Why do animals eat their meat raw?

Because they are terrible cooks.

Why did the pig pee all over his pen?

He wanted to go hog wild.

What's another name for cow poop?

Beef patties.

What does pig poop smell like?

It stoinks!

What do dogs call vomit?

Second dinner.

What do you get from a nauseated cow?

Spoiled milk.

What smells like ham and filth?

Pig farts.

What's red, chunky, and smells like a gazelle?

Cheetah puke.

Which monster will make the biggest mess out of your bathroom?

The Loch Mess Monster.

What does a skunk say when you turn it inside out?

"Ouch!"

What gets better with age?

Dog poop.

What does bear poop smell like?

Unbearable.

What did the circus monkey say when the clown farted?

Nothing . . . it smelled so funny he couldn't stop laughing long enough to say anything!

What do you call a dinosaur that farts too much?

Stinky-saurus.

How do chickens know it's time to poop?

They use a cluck.

What cat loves beans the most?

Puss n' toots.

What do dogs call it when they poop in their crate?
Midnight snack.

What are grizzly bear farts like?
Silent but violent.

Why do horses fart when they gallop?
They wouldn't achieve full horsepower if they didn't.

Why didn't the pig laugh at the loud fart?

Because he was being a real boar.

What is orange and smells like peanuts?

Elephant puke.

How did the skunk feel after being run over by a car?

Smelly and tired.

What's brown, jumps, and lives in Australia?

Kangapoo.

What is a fly's favorite dessert?

Cow pie.

Two girls were walking in the woods. They came across a pile of dog poop. "Is that dog poop?" the first girl asked. "Smells like dog poop," said the other. Then they both put their finger in it. "Feels like dog poop." Then they both said, "Tastes like dog poop. Good thing we didn't step in it!"

Why did the vampire eat the dog?

He loves pupperonis.

What do cows read when they're in the bathroom?

Cattle-logs.

What's invisible and smells like carrots and cabbage?

Rabbit farts.

Why did the cheetah eat the gazelle?

Because he loves fast food.

What do dogs call rabbit poop?

Easter eggs.

What do you call an elephant in a toilet bowl?

Stuck.

Did you hear about the girl who found electric eels in her toilet?

It was a shocking discovery!

How did the T-Rex feel after vomiting all night?

Dino-sore.

How do you make a pig fly?

Feed it a bowl of beans.

What do you call it when a dinosaur urinates?

Pee-rex.

What do cows pee?

Cheese Whiz.

Have you heard the one about the constipated lion?

Get ready to roar!

What's the most gassy fish in the ocean?
Puffer fish.

What did the skunk say to the farting man?

"No need to make such a stink, I've got you covered."

What should you do if pigs start to fly?

Get an umbrella.

Two bats hanging in their cave. The first bat asked the second, "Do you remember the worst day of your life?" The second bat replied, "Yeah. The day I had diarrhea!"

What do you call poop you can't push out?

A frightened turtle.

Why was the crocodile's pee so yellow?

He drank too much gator-ade.

A bird in the hand . . . will probably poop in your hand.

What animal is best at wiping itself clean?

An octopus.

Did you hear about the turkey with a flatulence problem?

It shot stuffing all the way across the Thanksgiving table.

How is a scientist like a fly?

They are both attracted to stools.

Why did the bear throw up after eating George Washington?

Because it is hard to keep a good man down.

Where do pigs "do their business"?

In a pork-a-potty.

What's green, slimy, and smells like peanuts?

Elephant puke.

Why did the pig farmer go to the hospital?

He caught a bad case of pink eye.

Why do fish record how much they pooped?

They always have scales.

Why did the turkey need a bath?

It smelled fowl.

Did you hear about the T-rex that didn't have the ability to fart?

It faced ex-stink-tion.

What animal always throws up after it eats?

A yak.

Did you hear about the sheep that went to the bathroom together?

They were tightly knit.

What is a vampire's favorite dog breed?
Bloodhound.

Why did the sick chicken cross the road?

To get to the odor side.

Did you hear about the cow with diarrhea?

It was an udder disaster!

Why did the Loch Ness monster eat the ship?

He was craving Captain Crunch.

7
KNOCK, KNOCK, ANYBODY IN THERE?

Knock-knock!

Who's there?

Throat.

Throat who?

Throat out that sandwich; it's covered in boogers.

Knock-knock!

Who's there?

Pooh.

Pooh who?

Pooh-lease stop farting in the kitchen!

Knock-knock!

Who's there?

Butternut.

Butternut who?

Butternut sit in that steaming pile of diarrhea I just made!

Knock-knock!

Who's there?

Noah.

Noah who?

Noah were the bathroom is? I'm about to blow!

Knock-knock!
Who's there?
Fanny.
Fanny who?
Fanny'body knocks, tell them I'm going to be in here awhile.

Knock-knock!
Who's there?
Jamaica.
Jamaica who?
Jamaica mess in this bathroom?

Knock-knock!
Who's there?
Dismay.
Dismay who?
Dismay be the last time I'll let you use my toilet.

Knock-knock!
Who's there?
Ike.
Ike who?
Ike can't help but pee a little bit when I poop.

Knock-knock!
Who's there?
Mage.
Mage who?
Mage ya laugh so hard you peed yourself.

Knock-knock!
Who's there?
Who.
Who who?
Who flushed that poor owl down the toilet? I can hear it from here!

Knock-knock!

Who's there?

Wet.

Wet who?

Wet smells so bad?

Knock-knock!

Who's there?

Juicy.

Juicy who?

Juicy a plunger anywhere around here?

Knock-knock!

Who's there?

Megan.

Megan who?

Megan logs in the toilet!

Knock-knock!

Who's there?

Peas.

Peas who?

Peas pass the soap; I got something on my finger.

Knock-knock!

Who's there?

Interrupting fart.

Interrupting—

(*make* fart noise)

Knock-knock!

Who's there?

My.

My who?

My tissues can't clean this mess up!

Knock-knock!

Who's there?

Candy.

Candy who?

Candy farting please stop now?

Knock-knock!

Who's there?

Harry.

Harry who?

Harry up, I need to get to the toilet!

Knock-knock!

Who's there?

Dwayne.

Dwayne who?

Dwayne the tub; I need to use the toilet!

Knock-knock!

Who's there?

Figs.

Figs who?

Figs the toilet! You clogged it.

Knock-knock!
Who's there?
Esther.
Esther who?
Esther a doctor on call? My diarrhea is out of control!

Knock-knock!
Who's there?
Europe.
Europe who?
No, you're a poo!

Knock-knock!
Who's there?
Urine.
Urine who?
Urine luck! The bathroom's open.

Knock-knock!
Who's there?
Ooze.
Ooze who?
Ooze gonna clean up this toilet?

Knock-knock!
Who's there?
Manuel.
Manuel who?
Manuel be sorry if you don't start flushing the toilet!

Knock-knock!
Who's there?
Noah.
Noah who?
Noah any good laxatives?

Knock-knock!
Who's there?
Freddy.
Freddy who?
Freddy or not, I gotta go!

Knock-knock!
Who's there?
Bean.
Bean who?
Bean forgetting to put the seat down, haven't you?

Knock-knock!
Who's there?
Hewlett.
Hewlett who?
Hewlett the seat up?

Knock-knock!

Who's there?

Arthur.

Arthur who?

Arthur any plumbers on duty? Cuz we're gonna need one!

Knock-knock!

Who's there?

Esther.

Esther who?

Esther any more toilet paper?

Knock-knock!

Who's there?

Kent.

Kent who?

Kent you see this bathroom is occupied?

Knock-knock!

Who's there?

Aida.

Aida who?

Aida whole can of beans and I'm ready to empty the gas tank.

Knock-knock!

Who's there?

Europe.

Europe who?

European on my shoes!

Knock-knock!

Who's there?

Mop.

Mop who?

Stinks, huh?

Knock-knock!

Who's there?

Candice.

Candice who?

Candice bathroom smell any worse?

Knock-knock!
Who's there?
Stopwatch.
Stopwatch who?
Stopwatch you're doing and clean up this bathroom!

Knock-knock!
Who's there?
Dewey.
Dewey who?
Dewey really have to share this bathroom?

Knock-knock!
Who's there?
Needle.
Needle who?
Needle little help finding a bathroom?

Knock-knock!
Who's there?
Water.
Water who?
Water you doing in there? Hurry up and pee!

Knock-knock!

Who's there?

Will.

Will who?

Will you get me a tissue? It's dribbling into my mouth.

Knock-knock!

Who's there?

Wanna.

Wanna who?

No, thanks, I'm fine.

Knock-knock!

Who's there?

Blue.

Blue who?

Why are you crying? It was only a fart.

Knock-knock!
Who's there?
Iva.
Iva who?
Iva sore butt from that bathroom trip.

Knock-knock!
Who's there?
Butfor.
Butfor who?
Butfor pooping!

Knock-knock!
Who's there?
Diploma.
Diploma who?
Diploma is here to fix the toilet.

Knock-knock!

Who's there?

Norma Lee.

Norma Lee who?

Norma Lee I don't leave such a stink in the bathroom. Apologies.

Knock-knock!

Who's there?

Rhino.

Rhino who?

Rhino you're the one that farted.

Knock-knock!

Who's there?

Bernie.

Bernie who?

Bernie candle; it stinks in here!

Knock-knock!
Who's there?
Watt.
Watt who?
Watt died in here?

Knock-knock!
Who's there?
A pile up.
A pile up who?
A pile up poo in the toilet? You better flush!

Knock-knock!
Who's there?
Pea.
Pea who?
Pea yew, what did you eat?

Knock-knock!

Who's there?

Donna.

Donna who?

Donna forget to flush when you're done in there!

Knock-knock!

Who's there?

Distinct.

Distinct who?

Distinct when you come out of the bathroom is disgusting.

Knock-knock!

Who's there?

Howard.

Howard who?

Howard you like to turn on a fan after what you just did to the bathroom?

Knock-knock!
Who's there?
Hyper.
Hyper who?
Hyper to use the bathroom at home.

Knock-knock!
Who's there?
Sherwood.
Sherwood who?
Sherwood be nice if you'd bring me something to read because I'm going to be in here awhile.

Knock-knock!
Who's there?
Butter.
Butter who?
Butter not tell you what I just did in the bathroom.

Knock-knock!

Who's there?

Justin.

Justin who?

Justin time to make it to the bathroom, whew!

Knock-knock!

Who's there?

Madam.

Madam who?

Madam toilet won't flush!

Knock-knock!

Who's there?

Bogey.

Bogey who?

Bogey hangin' from your nose!

Knock-knock!
Who's there?
Honey.
Honey who?
Honey would you please flush the toilet when you're done in there?

Knock-knock!
Who's there?
Abbott.
Abbott who?
Abbott time we got a candle for this bathroom!

Knock-knock!
Who's there?
Hoof.
Hoof who?
Hoof farted?

Knock-knock!
Who's there?
Hugh.
Hugh who?
Hugh shat all over the bathroom and forgot to clean it up?

Knock-knock!

Who's there?

Termite.

Termite who?

Termites the night I can finally go poo, thanks to these laxatives!

Knock-knock!

Who's there?

Cara.

Cara who?

Cara me to a toilet; I'm gonna spew!

Knock-knock!

Who's there?

Don.

Don who?

Don think you can get away with peeing on the seat again!

Knock-knock!

Who's there?

Bella.

Bella who?

Bella button lint tastes great!

Knock-knock!
Who's there?
Alda.
Alda who?
Alda potato salad got spoiled. The bathroom will be toxic!

Knock-knock!
Who's there?
Chuck.
Chuck who?
Chuck your pants; I think that fart went rogue.

Knock-knock!
Who's there?
Yule.
Yule who?
Yule be sorry if you make another round to that buffet.

Knock-knock!
Who's there?
Namir.
Namir who?
Namir earwax, better eat some belly button lint!

Knock-knock!
Who's there?
Maggot.
Maggot who?
Maggot snappy in there! I gotta go number two!

Knock-knock!
Who's there?
Pencil.
Pencil who?
Pencil be stained if you keep making those juicy farts!

Knock-knock!
Who's there?
Stan.
Stan who?
Stan back. I'm about to spew!

Knock-knock!
Who's there?
Gas.
Gas who?
Gas who stunk up the bathroom!?

Knock-knock!
Who's there?
Hank.
Hank who?
Hank you for turning on the fan in the bathroom!

Knock-knock!
Who's there?
Omar.
Omar who?
Omar god, these farts are horrible!

Knock-knock

Who's there?

Sausage.

Sausage who?

Sausage a mess you left in that bathroom.

Knock-knock

Who's there?

Joanne.

Joanne who?

Joanne's need to get cleaned after that bathroom visit.

8
DOCTOR, DOCTOR!

What's the nastiest habit a proctologist can have?

Nailbiting.

Why did the banana go to the doctor?
It wasn't peeling well.

Why did the kid with food poisoning have to stay at home?
It was doctor's odors.

A doctor handed a patient a specimen cup and said, "You can go fill this up in there," pointing to the bathroom. A few minutes later, the patient came out and handed the empty cup to the doctor. "I didn't need this. There was a toilet in there, so I used that."

How can you tell if a book was written by a proctologist?
Lots and lots of colons.

Man: *Doctor, you gotta help me! Every morning when I wake up and look in the mirror, I throw up. What's wrong with me?*
Doctor: *I'm not sure, but your eyesight is perfect.*

Patient: *Doctor, I need a medication for constipation.*

Doctor: *Here you are, sir. This is the #1 doctor rated laxative on the market.*

Patient: *That's great, but I'd really prefer the #2.*

Why did the bacon go to the hospital?

It wanted to be cured.

Man: *Doctor, I'm having trouble breathing.*

Doctor: *Don't worry, we will soon put a stop to that!*

What did the Doctor say to the witch?

"Warts the problem?"

Why did the Dr. prescribe acne medication to the teenager?

Because he was seeing spots.

Doctor: *Ma'am, I'm afraid I have some bad news. You have a hard time paying attention, as well as severe diarrhea.*

Woman: *Oh dear, well at least I don't have severe diarrhea.*

Man: *Doctor! I have a piece of lettuce peeking out of my anus!*

Doctor: *That's troubling. This just the tip of the iceberg.*

Did you hear about the dentist who diagnosed his patient's bad breath?

The patient was in the waiting room at the time.

Why did the dumb guy bring a chair to his doctor?

They said he needed to bring in a stool sample.

Did you hear about the guy who went to Costco and then went to the doctor?

First he got free samples and then he left pee samples.

Patient: *Doctor, doctor, you gotta help me!*
Doctor: *What seems to be the problem?*
Patient: *There's a big crack in my butt!*

Did you know the residents of Belgium have some of the worst allergies in the world?

They're all Phlegmish.

Did you hear about the astronomer
whose pants fell down?

It was a full moon.

Did you hear about the astronomer with saggy pants?
It was a half moon.

Patient: *Doctor, I'd like to treat my hemorrhoids. Do you have any articles or research I can read?*
Doctor: *Piles!*

A proctologist goes out to dinner one night, and a waiter comes to take his order. He notices the waiter keeps scratching his butt. The proctologist asks, "Do you have hemorrhoids?" The waiter replies, "We've only got what's on the menu."

Patient: *Doctor, you gotta help me. I think I've got hemorrhoids.*
Doctor: *Swell!*

Patient: *Doctor, you gotta help me. I've got a massive pain in the rear.*
Doctor: *Really? I've always liked your husband.*

Patient: *What did you think of my urine sample?*
Doctor: *Frankly, it was pee-utiful.*

Woman: *Doctor! My husband's farts smell like fish and I can't stand it!*
Doctor: *What a poor sole!*

What dessert should a proctologist
never bring to a potluck?

Chocolate cream pie.

Patient: Doctor my nose won't stop running?

Doctor: Just let it keep at it.
It will tire itself out soon.

Patient: Doctor! I keep making wind around my wife!

Doctor: Tell her to buy a kite.

Patient: *Doctor! I fart so loudly I keep myself awake at night!*

Doctor: *You should sleep in another room.*

Patient: *Doctor, these fart pills don't help at all! I'm still tooting.*

Doctor: *Which end did you put them in?*

Patient: *Doctor! People say my farts sound like a motorbike!*

Doctor: *You shouldn't let them rev you up.*

Why did the bowel movement go to the doctor?

It was always pooped.

Patient: *Doctor! I have a problem! Every morning, I poop at 7 on the nose!*

Doctor: *How is that a problem?*

Patient: *I get up at 9!*

What did the doctor give the
toilet with a sore throat?

Dima -crap.

Hard-of-hearing Harold and his loud wife Joan went to the doctor. "I am going to need a urine and feces sample," the doctor said. To which Joan yelled, "HAROLD, HE NEEDS A PAIR OF YOUR UNDERWEAR!"

Patient: I need a pill to help me stop sleep walking!

Doctor: No. I'm afraid you need the exercise.

Patient: *Doctor! I need your help. When I eat chicken, chicken comes out of my bottom, and when I eat carrots, it comes out of my bottom too!*

Doctor: *There's a cure for that. Just eat poop.*

An old woman went to the doctor's office. "Doctor." she said in a raspy voice. "I have an issue with gas. I fart, but they're silent and never smell. How can you help me?" "Well," the doctor said. "Take one of these every morning." He handed the small bottle of pills to the lady. Next week, the lady came back and said, "Doctor! Now my farts smell horrible! What did you give me!" "Good, good. Now that your sinuses are clear, let's work on your hearing."

Doctor: *How have your bowel movements been?*

Patient: *Not great. The toilet's been broken, so I don't go as much, and things are really painful down there.*

Doctor: *Have you tried taking the plunger out of the toilet?*

Patient: *Doctor, I haven't pooped in weeks.*

Doctor: *Well, don't just sit there!*

Patient: *Doctor! I accidentally got a spoon stuck up there!*

Doctor: *Relax, don't make such a stir.*

Patient: *Doctor! could you please treat my toad?*

Doctor: *No, I'm afraid if I touch it, it will croak.*

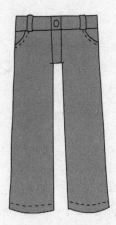

Patient: Doctor, I've got uncontrollable diarrhea. What should I do?

Doctor: Wear brown pants.

Patient: Help, doctor, my daughter just swallowed a pen. What should I do?

Doctor: Well, you probably aren't going to want to use that pen anymore.

Patient: *Doctor! I think I'm gonna hurl!*

Doctor: *What have you eaten today?*

Patient: *I've eaten two red licorices, three yellow taffies, and four blue ribbon candies.*

Doctor: *It's no wonder! You haven't been getting enough greens.*

Patient: *Doctor, you gotta help me. I eat apples, I see apples in the toilet later. I eat bananas, and nothing but bananas comes out.*

Doctor: *Have you tried eating poop?*

What does the queen do after she goes to the bathroom?

Makes a royal flush.

What do you get if you accidently dribble urine on the floor?

A mop!

What did the computer programmer say before going to the bathroom?

Excuse me, I need to check my IP address.

What is the quickest way to become European?

Go to the bathroom.

How did the toddler get such big muscles?

He was using pull-ups every night.

Why did the lawn go to the bathroom?

Because it needed a sprinkle.

Why did the man like his toilet paper so much?

Because it was Charmin'.

Why do men take showers instead of baths?

Because peeing in the bathtub is gross!

How do you know if you've embarrassed a toilet?

It flushes.

Why did the star go to the bathroom?

It needed to twinkle.

What smells like asparagus but tastes WAY worse than asparagus?

Asparagus pee.

Why did the plumber pee on his shoes?

He wanted to work from home.

Why did the barber use the alley on the way to the bathroom?

He liked making short cuts.

What's the biggest toilet in the world?
The Superbowl.

I GOTTA TAKE A LEAK!

Oh come on, you can do better than that. Here are a few alternatives.

• *Checking my fluid levels*

• *Raising the water level*

• *Paying the water bill*

• *Paying the piper*

- *Recycling some beverages*

- *Making an addition to the water table*

- *Putting out a fire*

- *Making it rain*

- *Shaking the dew off the flowers*

- *Check to see if the plumbing is working correctly*

What's a toilet's serial number?

4U2PN.

Which nut is always in the bathroom?

A pee-can.

Why did the man go into the restroom marked "Women"?

Because he couldn't read.

Have you ever heard of an ool?

It's a pool with no pee in it; they're very rare!

What did the mama say to the boy that peed on the rose bushes?

Urine trouble.

Boy: *Can I go to the bathroom?*

Teacher: *Only if you can sing the alphabet.*

Boy: ABCDEFGHIJKLMNOQRSTUVWXYZ

Teacher: *Where's the P?*

Boy: *Halfway down my leg!*

Every day at five o'clock, thousands of people rush home to use the toilet. It's flush hour!

How do you wash your hands with a urinal?
Use the soap at the bottom.

What did the plumber say to his apprentice?

Urine for a surprise.

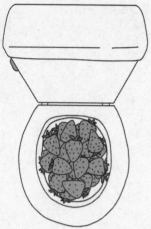

What do you call a bunch of
strawberries clogging up a toilet?

A real jam.

What's on a roll every day?

Toilet paper!

Does your grandpa have to wear disposable underwear?

Depends.

I am something in your bathroom.
I am found on a roll.
I am made to clean you.
Every time I'm used, I get dropped into a bowl.
What am I? . . . Toilet paper.

PEE-EW (WAYS TO SAY PEE)

- Sun showers

- Bitter lemonade

- Mountain Dew

- Mellow Yellow

- Recycled apple juice

- Emptying the bladder before there's a splatter

- Liquid sunshine

- Brine without the pickles

What do you call a cow's pee?
Cheese Whiz.

Why did the mummy not make
it to the bathroom in time?

He took too long to get unwrapped.

What's the difference between boiling eggs and pea soup?

Anyone can boil eggs.

What bathroom item is the biggest rip off?

Toilet paper.

What is the most refreshing thing to do when you pee?

Crack open a soda poop.

Why did the plumber quit his job?

He was tired of getting calls about leaks in the bathroom.

What did the toilet seat say about the messy man?

"It's so nice of him to always leave something behind."

What did Elsa sing while she was on the toilet?

"Let it flow, let it flow . . ."

A hike is just taking a walk in nature's bathroom.

What's the wettest nation on Earth?

Urination.

What are relief maps for?

Finding the bathroom.

How does urine get out of the body?

It climbs a bladder.

How do you know you've had one too many sodas?

When your pee is fizzy.

What days of the week is your urine stream at its strongest?

Saturdays and Sundays. All the others are just weak days.

Why is the weather in England so wet?

Because the Queen has reigned there for 64 years.

Which of the Great Lakes has the most pee in it?

Lake Urine. (Huron).

What does a baseball player say when he goes to the bathroom?

Bladder up.

What do you call it when you urinate on a golf course?

A tee-pee.

Why didn't Shakespeare make it to the bathroom in time?

Because he couldn't decide whether to pee, or not to pee.

What did the man say after he peed in the forest?

"Tree whiz!"

Do you want to join the pee club?

Congratulations, urine!

What's the worst part about using an office bathroom?

The paperwork.

What do you call a person who pees too much?

A wizz-ard.

What's the difference between pineapple and a diaper?

One is full of Ps and one is full of pee.

Why should you never eat a banana peel?

Because it's mostly pee.

What's the best thing about swimming in the ocean?

Nobody will notice if you pee a little.

What do you call a really expensive chair that smells like pee?

A throne.

How do you know you go to the bathroom too much?

You consider "10,000 Flushes" to be a challenge.

What do they call urinals in Russia?

Yuri-nals.

How do you make sure you don't get a baby shower?

Be alert when you change his diaper.

Which teacher made the biggest splash?

The PE teacher.

What do you call a man that flushes the toilet?

So-flush-sticated.

Where does Harry Potter go to the bathroom?

The headquarters at the Order of the Peenix.

What's the worst-tasting cake in the world?

A urinal cake.

Why does a beach smell like urine?

Because the sea weed.

Why did the man leave the bathroom?

He turd enough of the stall next to him.

What do you say to someone who's been throwing up all day long?

"Happy Barf-Day!"

Did you hear about the man who couldn't stop pooping and vomiting at the same time?

It's a pretty sick joke.

What do Italians call vomiting?

Barf-a-roni.

What happened to the teenager that drank eight sodas?

He threw 7 Up.

What machine plays music so bad
it makes you want to vomit?

A pukebox.

What color is a belch?

Purple.

How does a burp cut loose and get a little crazy?

It goes out the other end.

What's soft and warm at bedtime but hard and stiff in the morning?

Vomit.

What did ancient Romans do in a vomitorium?

Un-wine.

Did you hear about the guy who missed the puke bucket and vomited all over the floor?

It was beyond the pail!

Did you hear about the professional golfer that was so nervous about the tournament that he threw up?

Suppose it's just barf for the course.

I just can't help telling jokes about vomiting.
What can I say, it's a sickness!

What do poets do in the bathroom?

They write poo-ems.

Do you want to hear a joke about vomit?
Coming right up!

Did you hear about the pilot who barfed on the plane?
He got through it with flying colors.

This is the last joke about vomiting.
I promise not to bring that up anymore.

Where is the most entertaining place to puke?

A hot air balloon...
Not so entertaining for anyone else though.

Why did the criminal enjoy vomiting?

Because it's ill-egal.

What is the most nauseating city?

Barf-celona.

How can you tell the difference between a healthy dog and a sick dog?

One barks, the other barfs.

Funny Puke Names

Liquidation sale

Spew

Tossing cookies

Lunch summons

Retching

Making stew

Feeding Poseidon

Porcelain offering

Pit stop at regurgitation station

Upchuck

Hurling

Liquid moan

Making monster food

Horking

Visiting the ejection seat

Blowing chunks

Yelling for Ralph

The ol' heave ho

Chunder

Chili storm

Blowing beans

Hugging the toilet

Hit the eject button

The urp burp

The technicolor yawn

What do dogs call their own vomit?

The soup course.

What did a burp say to the other?

Let's be stinkers and go backwards.

What's small, cuddly, and green?
A koala that needs to puke.

What beats throwing up out of a speeding car window?

Your heart.

Did you hear about the girl that puked up her lunch into the bowl?

No? I'll spare you.

What's worse than eating vomit soup?

Eating day-old vomit soup.

What airline does everyone get sick on?

Spew-nited.

What does a competitive eater do in the bathroom?

Prepares for battle.

Why wouldn't the billionaire take a shower?

Because she was filthy rich.

What happened when the kindergartener got sick during fingerprinting class?

She made a retch-a-sketch.

What did the chef say to the toilet?

One dinner, coming right up!

What do you get when you eat asparagus and cabbage?

The worst smelling bathroom of all time.

What flavor of ice cream will make you sick?

Van -illa.

HAVE A FRIEND CELEBRATING A BARFDAY? HELP THEM GET INTO THE PARTY MOOD BY SINGING THIS SONG!

Happy barf day to you

You sat in my spew

Now you smell like vomit

Happy barf day to you

How did the bucket know he was about to vomit?
He was looking a little pail.

What's the best way to avoid getting sick in the car?

Roll down the window.

What's the difference between puke and school lunch?

School lunch comes on a plate.

What does Thor wear on his bottom?
Thunderpants.

Why did the girl get sick at the haunted house?
It was too spew-key.

What stinks and flies through the air at 500 mph?
An airplane bathroom.

What do you call a bathroom in Finland?
Helstinki.

Clever ways to tell someone that they REALLY need to take a shower:

• *You smell worse than a city dump full of dog poop.*

• *You smell like you ate a big bowl of farts for lunch.*

• *You smell like you forgot to take off every diaper you wore when you were a baby.*

• *You smell like you forgot to throw away the toilet paper when you were done with it.*

• *You smell like you took a dump instead of leaving it behind.*

• *A gas station bathroom would think you smell bad.*

• *You smell like a cat confused you for a litter box.*

• *You make natural gas seem like anything but natural.*

• *You smell like a fart and poop had a race to see who could get out first, and they tied.*

• *Did you burp out of your butt and fart out of your mouth at the same time?*

Disgusting Titles Coming Soon to a Bookshelf Near You!

The Diarrhea Family *by Manny Luce-Bowles*

Dealing with Constipation *by U. R. Stuck*

How to Be a Proctologist *by Seymour Butz*

How to Properly Clean Yourself *by Duke E. Viper*

A History of Plumbers' Pants *by Sawyer Crack*

Vomiting Techniques *by Anya Neeze*

The Most Frequent Urination Problems *by P.P. de Ponce*

Common Rashes *by Mike Rauch-Burns*

Chronic Gas *by Ran Sidass*

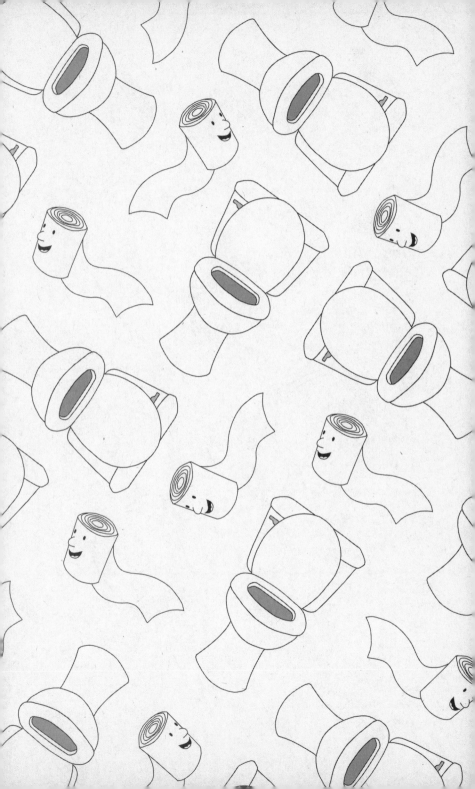